Blend Hunt

Set 6

Written by Kassi Gilmour

Practise the sounds

a b c d e f g h i j k l m n
o p qu r s t u v w x y z
ck wh ll ss ff zz th sh ch ng
oo oo th ai ee oa or er

The Blend Hunt books are designed to help children practise blending new sounds within each set. Once each word is successfully blended, children search for the item that matches the words they have read on each page.

Practise tricky words

to they of are have all her day
for like said what want saw be
were one some come

Blend Hunt

Set 6

Written by Kassi Gilmour

chi/cken

drink/er

perch

c	oa	l		t	r	ai	n

t	r	ee		t	u	nn	e	l

 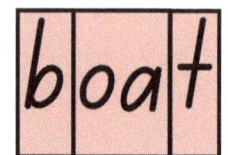

shel/ter   feed

grain

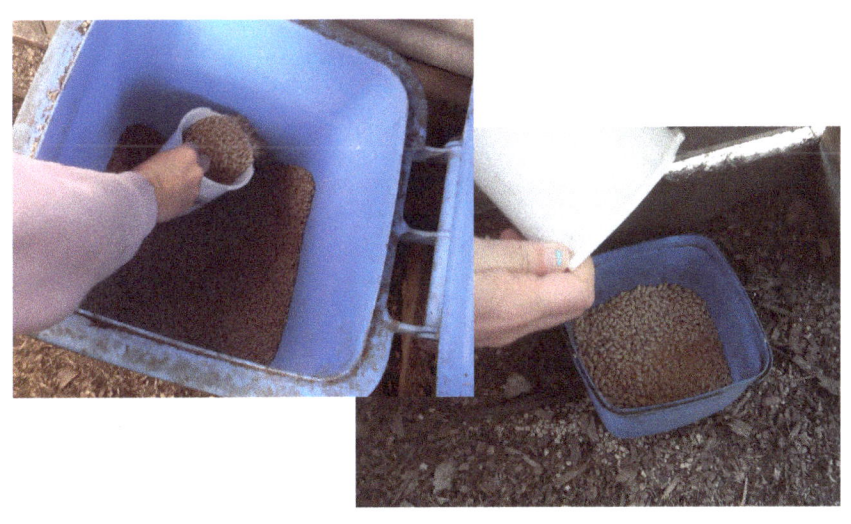

| s | ai | l | | p | or | t |

| l | oa | d | i | ng | | d | o | ck |

wooden boat float

roast pork

corn

rain|coat   lan|tern

t|or|ch

| p | la | t | f | or | m | | r | ai | l |

| w | ai | t | | t | i | ck | e | t | s |

pink tail

green shells

mer/maid un/der

coast

ri|v|er

f|l|oat

r|ee|l

Mermaid

Written by Kassi Gilmour

Practise the sounds

u l ll ss ff b j w wh y
th sh v qu z zz x
ch ng oo oo th
ai ee oa or er

Practise blending sounds

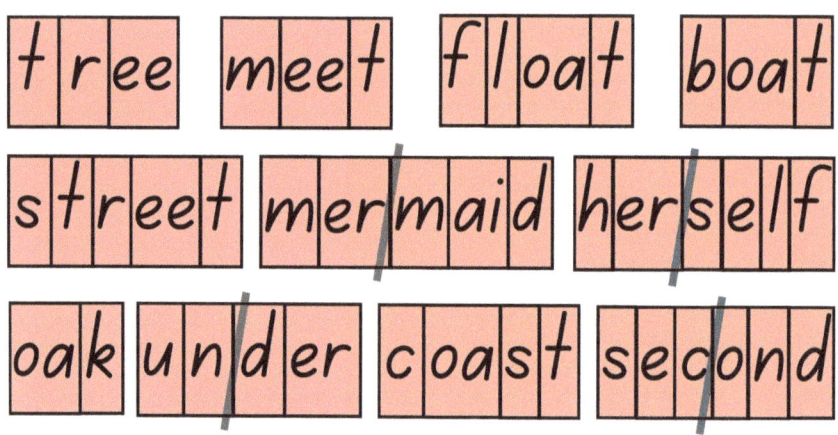

Practise tricky words

said what want saw be were one
some come little here there where
so put very down out

Mermaid

Set 6

Written by Kassi Gilmour

Pip likes the book, The Little Mermaid.

She wants to be a mermaid.

One day, Pip thinks, if I cannot be a mermaid, I want to meet one.

Pip strolls down the street to the coast.

She sits on a big rock under an old oak tree.

Pip looks and looks.

A boat floats out deep.

Pip sees a fin. "There is a mermaid!" she calls out.

It was not.

Pip sees a second fin.

That must be a mermaid, Pip thinks.

But, it was just a big fish.

Next, Pip sees a big fin. Is that a mermaid? Pip thinks.

No. It was not a mermaid.

Pip waits all day, but she has not seen a mermaid.

Do mermaids exist?
Pip thinks to herself.

It has been a long day, so
Pip will go back to her cabin.

Questions:

1. What story does Pip like?
2. Why does she go to the coast?
3. What does she see out at sea?
4. Were there any mermaids?
5. What is your favourite story?

Chickens

Written by Kassi Gilmour

Practise the sounds

u l ll ss ff b j w wh y

th sh v qu z zz x

ch ng oo oo th

ai ee oa or er

Practise blending sounds

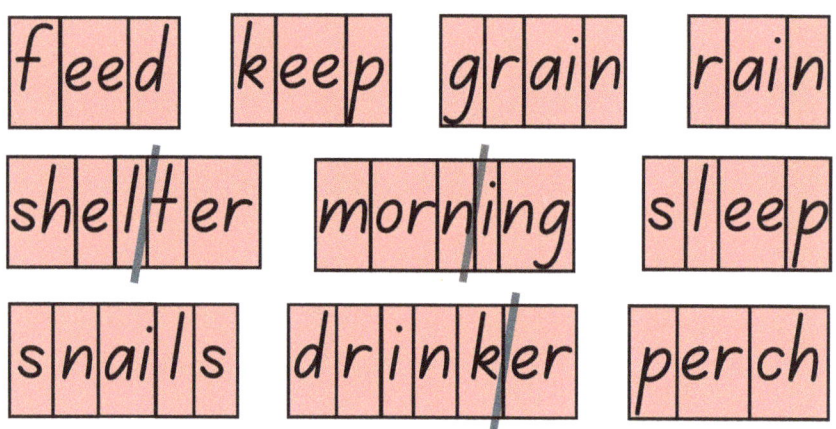

Practise tricky words

said what want saw be were

one some come little here there

where so put very down out

Chickens

Set 6

Written by Kassi Gilmour

We have chickens.

In the morning, mum feeds the chickens. She puts on her gum boots.

They have grain and scraps.

We keep the grain in a little bin so that the rats do not get it.

Chickens like snails and grubs, too.

We lift the lid on the nesting box to check for eggs.

When there are eggs, we collect them.

Chickens need to drink. We fill up the drinker.

Mum gets the chicken poo and puts it in a bucket.

She said that chicken poo feeds the plants, so she digs the poo into the planting beds.

Chickens need shelter from the rain. They have a little hut. We call it a chicken coop.

When the sun sets, the chooks roost on the perch.

They sleep there until the next day.

Chickens are very little and soft to pat.

We think they are good pets.

Questions:

1. Who looks after the chickens?
2. What do chickens need?
3. Where do they sleep?
4. Name 3 things you need to do for chickens?
5. Why do you think this family likes chickens?

Roast Dinner

Written by Kassi Gilmour

Practise the sounds

u l ll ss ff b j w wh y
th sh v qu z zz x
ch ng oo oo th
ai ee oa or er

Practise blending sounds

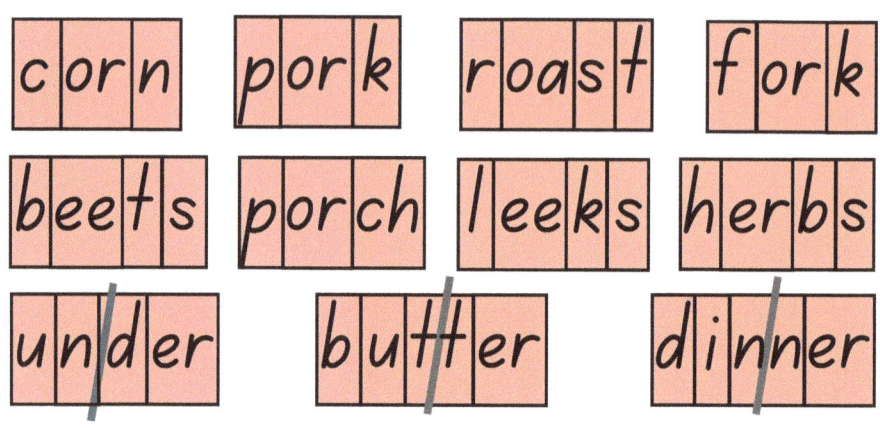

Practise tricky words

to day today said what want saw be
were one some come little here there
where so put very down out

Roast Dinner

Set 6

Written by Kassi Gilmour

On Sundays, Nan cooks a roast dinner for lunch.

Today, she will cook roast pork with herbs.

The sun is out, so Nan said we will have lunch on the porch.

It is my job to set up for lunch.

I put a cloth on and smooth it out.

Then, I put dishes, cups, forks and spoons out.

Next, I put some napkins under the cups.

Nan hands me some fresh rolls and butter.

They smell so good!

Nan brings out her cooking and puts it on the lunch bench.

She cuts the roast pork and puts some on my dish.

Then, Nan scoops out some corn, beets and leeks for me.

Next, I hold the tongs and get some hot chips.

We all sit down on the porch to have Nan's roast dinner.

I like Sunday lunch at Nan's. It is very yum!

Questions:

1. When does Nan cook roast lunches?
2. What did she cook?
3. What is the boy's job?
4. Why do you think he likes Sunday lunch?
5. Do you have special family dinners?

The Little Mermaid

Written by Kassi Gilmour

Practise the sounds

u l ll ss ff b j w wh y
th sh v qu z zz x
ch ng oo oo th
ai ee oa or er

Practise blending sounds

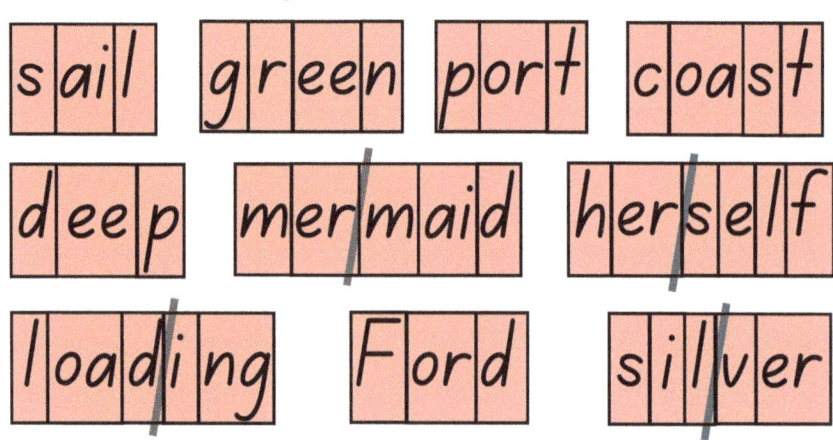

Practise tricky words

liked ago said what wanted saw be
were one some come little here
there where so put very down out

The Little Mermaid

Set 6

Written by Kassi Gilmour

Long ago, there was a little mermaid. She had a pink tail and green shells.

The little mermaid had a pet.
Her pet was Ford.

Ford liked to look for ships that had sunk.

Deep down, there were lost chests of gold and silver.

One day, the little mermaid said, "I want to visit the coast to see where the ships come from."

Ford did not think this was a good plan.

He told the little mermaid not to go, but she still went.

She swam to the coast. It was a long swim.

The next morning, the little mermaid got to the coast. She saw land and a loading dock in the port.

She saw tall ships with big sails in the port.

Men did not have tails, but had legs and feet. They were loading the ships.

An old wooden chest was put on a ship. "There must be gold and silver in that chest," the little mermaid said to herself.

Just then, the little mermaid's mum swam up next to her.

"What are you doing here?" her mum said.

"I wanted to see where the ships come from," the little mermaid told her mum.

Her mum said, "Let's swim back to Ford. He misses you."

Questions:

1. Describe the little mermaid.
2. Who is Ford?
3. Why do they like exploring shipwrecks?
4. Why does the little mermaid want to swim to the coast?
5. What does she see at the coast?
6. Do you think the little mermaid is happy that she saw where the ships came from?

Tait's Old Boat

Written by Kassi Gilmour

Practise the sounds

u l ll ss ff b j w wh y
th sh v qu z zz x
ch ng oo oo th
ai ee oa or er

Practise blending sounds

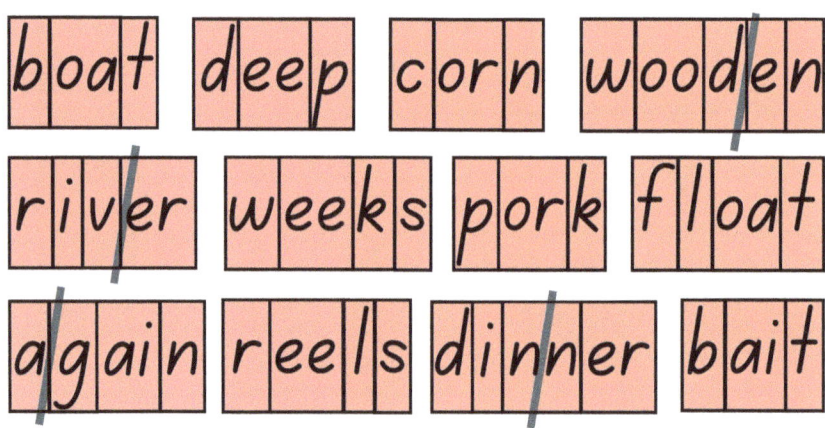

b|oa|t d|ee|p c|or|n w|oo|d|e|n
r|i|v|er w|ee|k|s p|or|k f|l|oa|t
a|g|ai|n r|ee|l|s d|i|nn|er b|ai|t

Practise tricky words

in<u>to</u> said what want saw be were
one some come little here there
where so put very down out

Tait's Old Boat

Set 6

Written by Kassi Gilmour

Tait has an old wooden boat.

He spent weeks fixing the old boat so it floats.

Tait wants to go fishing at the river.

Tait puts his boat in the river to test it. It floats!

He hops in and drifts out to where it is deep.

Tait puts bait on his hook and drops it into the river.

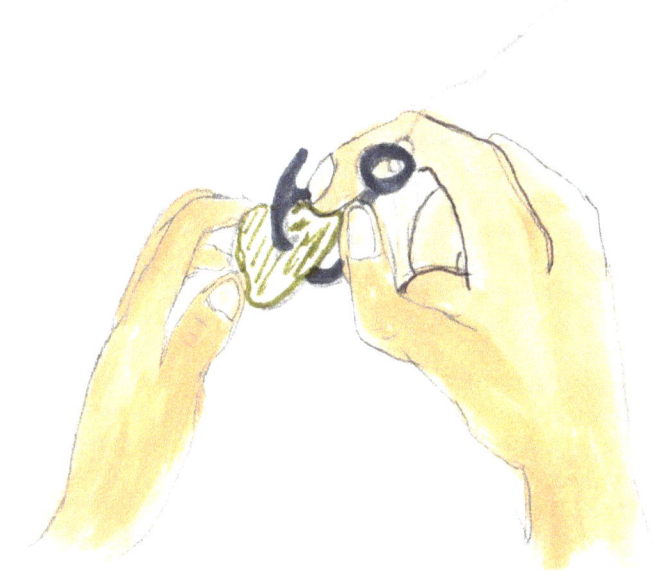

He waits and waits.

Tug! Tug! Tug!

Tait holds the rod and reels in...

...river reeds. "That is not what I want," Tait fusses.

Tait waits again.

Tug! Tug! Tug!

He reels in his hook to see...

...a short chain.

Tait has his lunch. It is pork and corn on a roll. Yum!

Then, he has a drink and keeps on fishing.

Tug! Tug! Tug!

Tait reels up...

...a fish!

The old wooden boat floats back to the land.

Tait will have fish for dinner.

Questions:

1. Why does Tait want a boat?
2. How long does Tait spend fixing his boat?
3. What did Tait catch while he was fishing?
4. How do you think Tait felt after he caught reeds and a short chain?
5. How did he feel at the end of the story?
6. What do you know about fishing?

Old Trains

Written by Kassi Gilmour

Practise the sounds

u l ll ss ff b j w wh y
th sh v qu z zz x
ch ng oo oo th
ai ee oa or er

Practise blending sounds

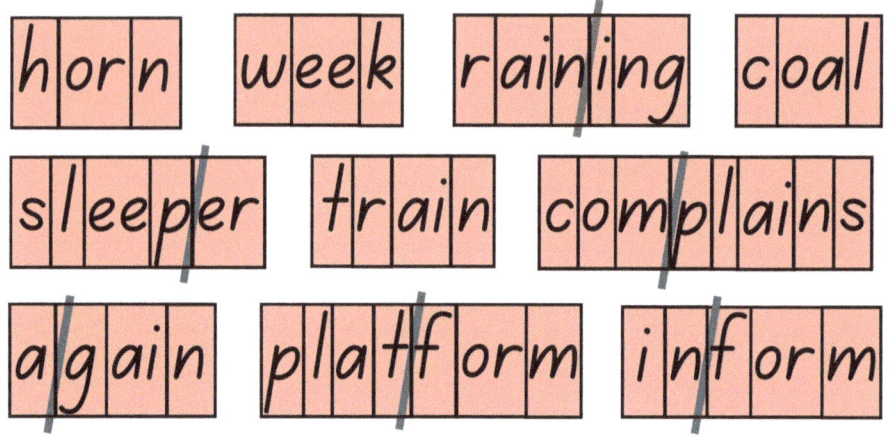

Practise tricky words

to day today a go ago said what want
saw be were one some come little here
there where so put very down out <u>about</u>

Old trains

Set 6

Written by Kassi Gilmour

"It is so wet!" Jill complains.

"Yes, and the rain will not stop," adds Jack.

Pop can see that Jack and Jill are sad. He gets an old book and sits with them.

"Long ago, trains ran on coal,"
Pop tells Jack and Jill.

He tells them lots of things about old trains.

"Pop, do old trains still run today?" Jill quizzes Pop.

Pop thinks for a bit.

"Yes, there are little trains that are like the old trains," Pop informs them.

"Can we see them?" Jack begs.

Pop tells Jack and Jill that they can go and see the little old trains next week, if it is not raining.

The next week, the sun was out.

"Pop, it is not raining! Can we go and see the little old trains today?" Jill begs.

"We need to pack lunch, and then we will go," Pop tells them.

When they get there, Jack sees a little train going on a very small track.

"The little wood sleepers hold the rails," Pop tells Jill.

Jill sees a man dig coal and put it in a little train. The horn honks and is very strong for such a little train.

Pop gets some tickets, and they wait on the platform.

The little train comes, and they hop on. "Here we go!" Jack calls out.

Chug! Chug! Chug! The little train runs on the rails. It chugs up and down little hills and into a tunnel.

"That was so much fun! Can we go again?" Jill begs Pop. He grins.

Questions:

1. At the beginning of the story, why are Jack and Jill sad?
2. How does Pop cheer them up?
3. When do they go to see the little trains?
4. What do they see at the little trains?
5. Have you ever been on a miniature train?

Storm

Written by Kassi Gilmour

Practise the sounds

u l ll ss ff b j w wh y
th sh v qu z zz x
ch ng oo oo th
ai ee oa or er

Practise blending sounds

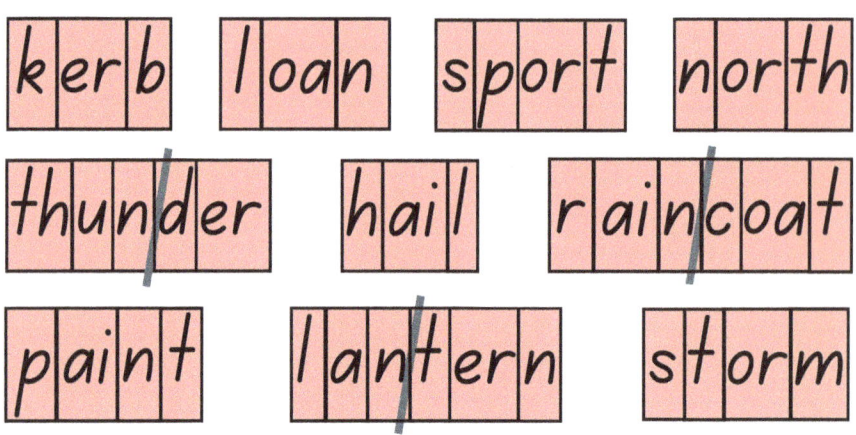

Practise tricky words

to day today all said what want saw
be <u>b</u>egins were one some come little
here there where so put very down out

Storm

Set 6

Written by Kassi Gilmour

I cannot go to football today.

All sports are off.

There is a big storm. The storm is north of us, but it will come down here soon.

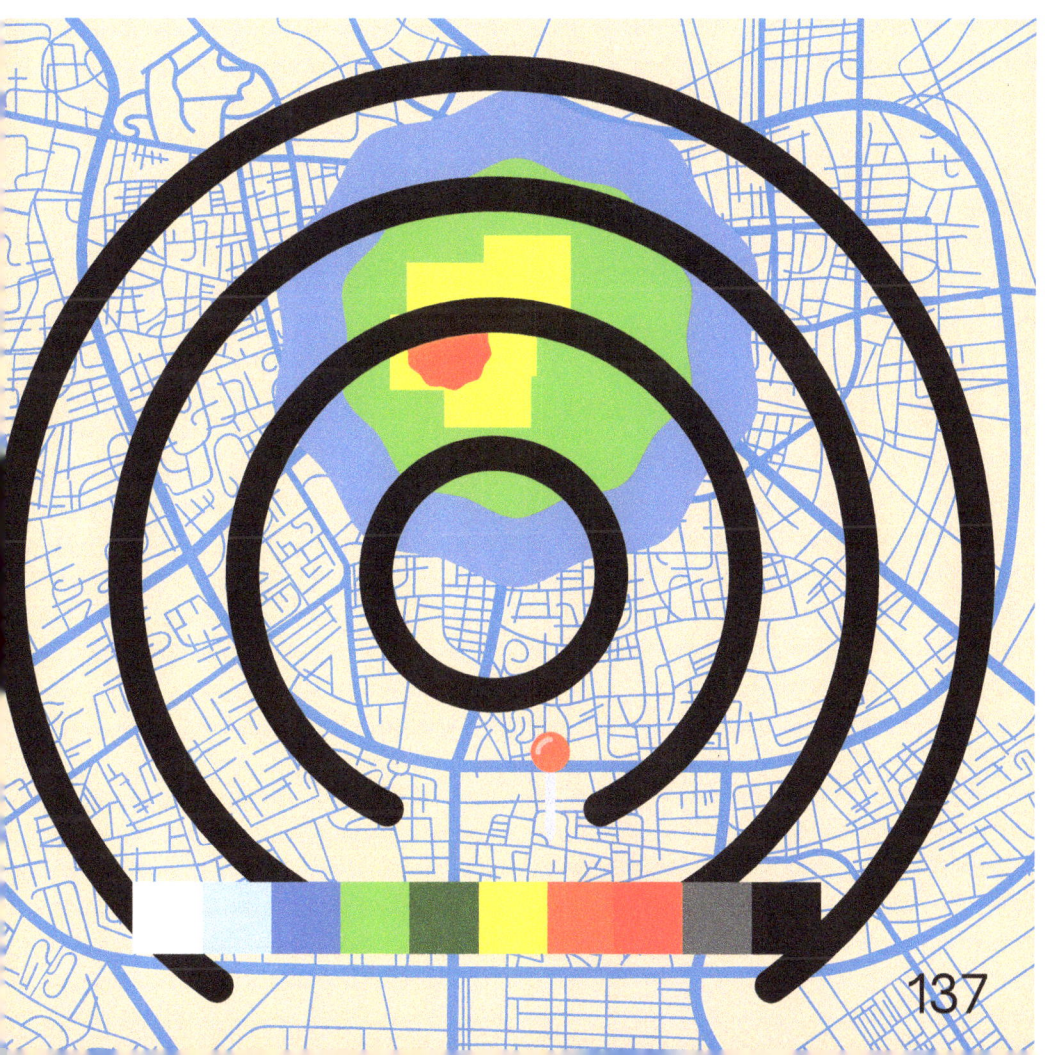

When it begins to rain, we bring the dog in.

Soon, lots of rain falls.

Then, some hail bangs on the roof.

Flashes paint the room.

Bang! There is a big clap of thunder.

"We have a blackout," said Dad. "We need a lantern."

"I will get the lantern," Mum said.

The lantern was old and worn out.

"I will go across the street and loan a torch," Dad said as he put on his raincoat.

Dad went to loan a torch from Max.

When Dad got back, his raincoat was soaking wet.

He hangs it up.

Dad holds the torch. We all sit down and look at books.

When the storm ends, Dad checks things.

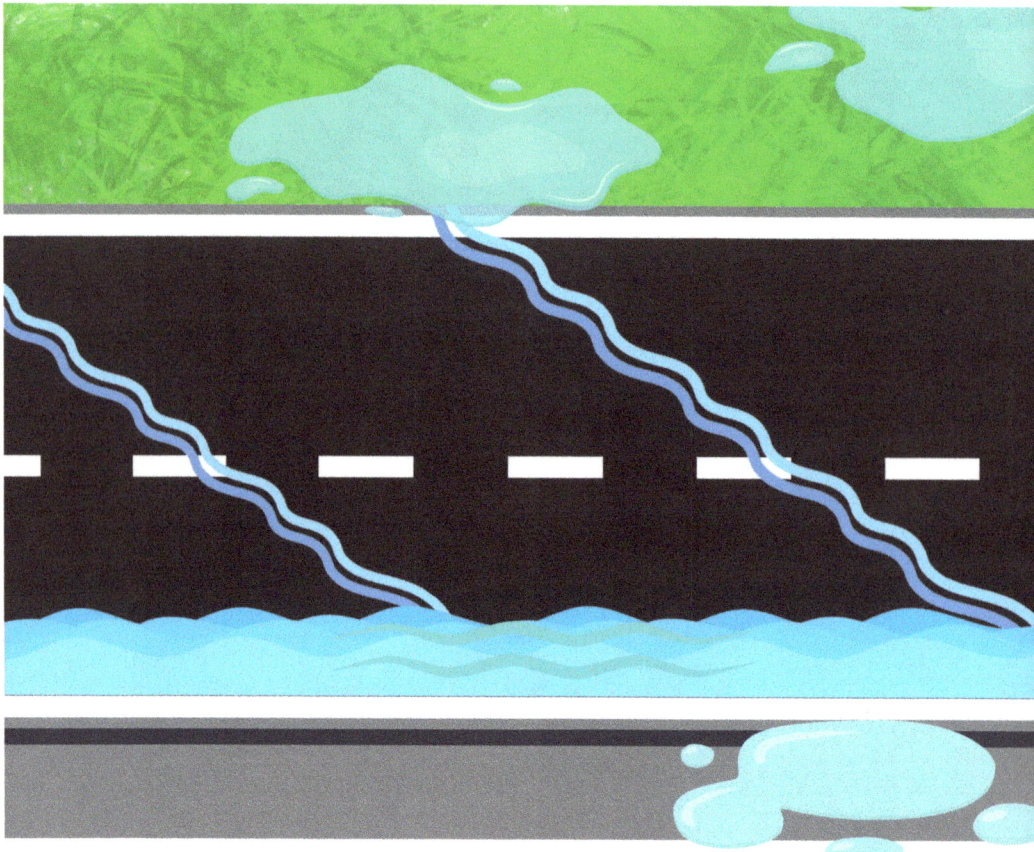

The kerb on the street is like a little river.

"That storm was short, but big," Mum said.

We are all glad the storm has come to an end.

Questions:

1. What sport does the boy play?
2. Why were all sports cancelled?
3. Where did the storm come from?
4. How was Dad helpful during the storm?
5. Have you ever been in a storm? Recall your experience.

www.ingramcontent.com/pod-product-compliance
Lightning Source LLC
Chambersburg PA
CBHW042131100526
44587CB00026B/4258